LOVE OVER FEAR

A Guide to Peace and Purpose

Monk Coleman

LOVE OVER FEAR

The book information is catalogued as follows;
Author Name(s): MONK COLEMAN
Title: LOVE OVER FEAR

Description; First Edition
1st Edition, 2021
Book Design by MICHAEL MALONEY

ISBN (paperback) 978-1-913479-76-3
ISBN (ebook) 978-1-913479-77-0

Published by That Guy's House
www.ThatGuysHouse.com

"Set down the heavy bags of the past. The baggage containing fear, doubt, and anger. Step through the threshold to the unlimited potential of the present and the future. Breathe. Live. Smile. Share. My good friend Monk has created an excellent handbook to provide all of us with simple reminders to live and love our life journey. Enjoy."

Eric D. Hobbs, Ph.D, CEO Berkeley Lights Inc.

"Most of us can grasp the simplicity of the choice between love and fear. But what Monk is calling for is not another meme-generated smile at the wisdom of the sages, but a call to action, a conscious practice of choosing love over fear. This compassionate connection to truth, takes our hand and walks us through what conscious living feels like. Monk's kindness and clarity in "Love Over Fear" help release us from the noise and distractions of the modern world, to re-remember who we are and why we are here - to love. Life does not come with an instructional manual, but it does provide the teachers, and I am eternally grateful for the guidance that Monk offers here."

Geoff Palmer CEO,Founder - Clean Machine - Plant Based Fitness Nutrition

"For several years, the person that I know as Monk has always been a great father, husband, health conscious, caring, and humble person set on an inspiring mission to help save the earth."

Lonnie Jordan, Lead singer, "WAR"

"I found Monk on Facebook some years back, and was immediately intrigued with what he had to say about his journey to becoming vegan. I had the opportunity to meet his beautiful wife Tammy when they attended one of my raw food events. Monk did an incredibly inspiring lecture that day at the event, and I've watched him excel and evolve over the years! My husband - Lonnie Jordan and I have become close friends with Monk and Tammy, and we feel so blessed having them in our lives."

Teresa Jordan, Raw Vegan Chef

"Monk Eternal! Let's start with the name. It says it all. Monk is a brotha, friend, colleague and my teacher. I have the divine privilege to walk the path of enlightenment with a true Urban Monk. I prayed, asking God to send a brotha to co-create and inspire the world, and the Universe sent me Monk Eternal. 'Love Over Fear' is a must read. If you are looking for direction and purpose, this is the book for you."

Rev Skip Jennings - Author, Minister,
Co-Host of 2 Black Authors

Acknowledgments

First of all, I'd like to thank Sean Patrick and Skip Jennings from That Guy's House publishing for making this all happen.

So many people have influenced me in one way or another, too many to name them all, but I'd like to thank you for playing a role in my growth and unfoldment.

To my wife, Tammy Coleman, for always being there during the challenging times, holding space, loving and supporting me through it all. I love you.

To my children, I love every last one of you. Demarcus, William, Olivia, Jake, Cedric, and Eshiana. You are all very special to me, and I thank you for everything you've taught me.

To my mother, Wanda Coleman, for loving us, making something out of nothing, and dealing with all seven of us hard-headed kids. Miracle worker! We love you.

To my friends, Teresa and Lonnie Jordan, thank you for seeing something in me that I didn't see in myself. Thank you for inviting me to L.A, to your home, for my first speaking engagement, ever. You were the catalyst for my speaking career when I didn't realize I was a speaker. I thank you so much for letting us into your world and accepting us into your tribe.

A special shout out and thank you to my little brother Juno Prince for coming through for me on many occasions when I was struggling out here, manifesting my dreams.

To my brothers from another Motha: Mario "Cat" Catley and Jamal "skinny boy" Collins, you are the real ones! You are a perfect example of what friends should be. Thank you.

To my brothers Chris Rodarte and Robert Cox, for hanging tough when we were running the streets, trying to find what we were looking for, but never finding it! Those years were tough for me, but I'm glad that I had partners like y'all to be there with me. I needed to experience those times so I can be the man I am today.

Dedication to Co-Contributors

To Jamal Collins and Shelby Chipelewski

In Life, you connect with other souls that enter your circle at precisely the right time. When inspiration hit me to start creating this book, and I began to write, I knew it was going to be critical in helping others shift from living a life of fear to one of Love. When I introduced my intention to Jamal and Shelby, they saw my vision and fully jumped in to help complete the book that is now called Love over Fear, a guide to peace and purpose. Thank you for all your hard work and dedication.

Contents

FOREWORD

It was a cool sunny Saturday in Eureka, Ca. The homies were hanging at the park listening to music on the beat box, drinking 40's, blazing, joking and thinking of our next move or come up. One of the homies brought with him a youngster named Joe, who is now known as Monk. Monk was a light skinned brother with a tightly-faded, razor sharp haircut, about 5'9, and maybe about 125lbs on a good day. The tightly faded haircut was what impressed me, due to the fact there was no barber shops in Humboldt county that catered to cutting black mens hair properly, so one needed to know a student from out of the area attending Humboldt State University or College of the Redwoods to get a proper haircut. The last thing a brother wants is a messed up haircut because you will hear about it from the homies. I asked Monk where he got his cut. Monk stated that he cuts his own hair. Monk was the real deal with the clippers and that is where our journey began.

Monk never had a problem with attracting the ladies, with his tank top t-shirt, pressed khakis and sense of humor. His smooth operator mentality always won them over. A few of these relationships created some of the most beautiful, brilliant minds.

Back then, Monk was just blowing in the wind, as we find ourselves at times. I would have never ever thought that Monk would be an author of a book and, even more ridiculous, a self-help book.

We partied hard together. We worked out together and played pick up ball together. We bought old school cars together. Our kids played together. We broke bread together. I looked at Monk as the little brother I never had.

I can remember the last time we drank together. We met at a bar in Berkeley and we both had beers. Monk was telling me that something was wrong with his stomach. Around that time, I believe the seeds of Monk's transformation were starting to grow. He focused on meditation, which eventually brought him to a plant based diet, and working out.

Monk went from vegetarian to vegan. I would call him the vegan pastor. The pastor sometimes you don't like to see because he wants to convert you that day, that moment. I realized when you care about someone, to encourage positive change, their truth and reality align.

"What lies behind us and what lies before us are tiny matters compared to what lies within us." ~ Ralph Waldo Emerson

This positive lifestyle change is working for Monk and he has found his way. The beautiful thing about it is Monk is showing others everyday the steps to find theirs. What are your tools for life? What is your life language? And what is living your best life? If you haven't found them yet, the answers to these questions and much more are pages away for your discovery.

Sherman Landry

Employment & Training Program, Coordinator - Dept. of Health & Human Services

MY STORY

I just touched down in Miami. I'm ready for a week of partying - late nights and early mornings. You know that Miami Life? That night, I had just found out that I was going to have another baby, and I was ready to go big as usual. I never did my partying halfway. I was always the first to start and the last to end. The first night, I stayed up drinking and smoking until about 6 am. I got up to go to the bathroom, and I realized I was peeing blood - "what the hell?" This was the beginning of the end of my old life as I knew it. This was the beginning of the end of living my life in the basement.

What is Life in the basement, you might ask? "Life in the basement" is the experiences you have when you're not living in your truth or living your purpose. It's a life of confusion and wrong thinking. "Life in the basement" brings people and experiences into your life that seem to punish you. It's full of low vibrational experiences. It's dense, it's heavy, it's constricting. "Life in the basement" almost seems to be sucking the life out of you, and quite often, it does. Everyone doesn't live here, but everyone has experienced it at one time or another. If you choose to continue to live here (it is a choice) or to be a frequent visitor, very little in your Life will change for the better, and your growth will be minimal. You will not have the life that is your birthright, the Life that you deserve, that Life filled with peace, purpose, Love, and healthy relationships. When you came into existence on this earthly plane, you came here as a perfect expression of God… and you still are. The only thing that has changed is you don't realize this is still true. You've been lied to, manipulated, and conditioned to think otherwise. But don't be mistaken, "Life in the basement" serves a purpose. The Universe is working for you and never against you, so you must realize all your experiences are valuable learning tools. I would not be here where I am today if it weren't for the things I had to go through "in the basement". My most significant breakthroughs came at the lowest points in my life, and the lowest points happened there, of course. The question now is, are you ready to elevate? Are you tired of "in the basement" experiences? Are you ready to live the life you deserve? Are you tired of being tired? If the answer is YES, then this book is for you!

I came from a very poor family with six siblings and very few resources, so we had our challenges. My father passed away when I was around three years old (I was his only biological), which compounded my life at home. I do remember my father even though I was young. I remember that he loved me. My mother used to say, "he did a lot of things wrong, but he sure loved you". I never really thought about it much growing up, and I didn't think it had that much of an impact on me, but I found that to be the furthest from the truth. I realized that support or lack of support from a father, or father figure (I had neither), would have a lot to do with my trajectory in life.

There was definitely a void that needed to be filled. Even though I now know how important being there for your kids is, it didn't seem as necessary until I started to wake up. I wish I would have had this epiphany sooner. After my father passed, I realized that I didn't quite fit in, not even in my own family. My insecurities began to build as the years went on because I'd shut down a little more with each experience that solidified my negative beliefs about myself. This experience started me on a long, hard road to self-discovery (even though I didn't know that's what it was) with a lot of trial and error - mostly error. All my relationships failed miserably. I became an alcoholic, chose a life of crime, and was a womanizer. On top of all that, I obviously wasn't being the father I should be. I learned through all these roadblocks and hardships that I had to take FULL responsibility. I knew there was something else to life, but it was as if I was feeling my way in the dark, trying everything, hopelessly wishing for a miracle to bring me out of this depressing state.

How did I make my transformation? My father had struggled with drugs, alcohol, and from what I've heard, had a tendency towards violence. Now, it was me going down the same path, without a clue as to how I got there and feeling hopeless with no way of breaking this vicious cycle. Even though I was raised in organized religion, I quickly made my way to a life full of "the worst-case" scenarios and mistakes. I was putting myself in harm's way daily, not seeing the pattern that was right in front of my face; I was becoming my father.

My Life then came to a crossroads at thirty-eight years old. Through all the years of "partying" and abuse to my body, my body started to fail. It was a life or death decision, and I chose LIFE! Through meditation and spiritual practice, I finally discovered myself and all the limitless possibilities that were there for me.

In these trying times, it is imperative that we heal ourselves and collectively, to raise the collective consciousness to make way for a new world and way of living. I'm entirely on board, and I trust that this book can also be the impetus to jump start YOU to be on your way to a peaceful and purpose-filled life. I love you.

Monk Coleman

THE PRACTICE

LOVE OR FEAR IN ACTION

"There are two basic motivating forces: Fear and Love. When we are afraid, we pull back from Life. When we are in Love, we open to all that Life has to offer with passion, excitement, and acceptance."
John Lennon

"Step into the fire of self-discovery. This fire will not burn you, it will only burn what you are not."
Mooji Baba

"If Love is light, Fear is its Shadow"
L.J Vanier

We all operate on one of two emotions, Love or Fear. We are born with instincts driving us towards survival, and as a young child, we're told not to rebel. Don't talk back, don't question it, don't risk it. Fear creeps in when we forget to trust our intuition. We're here to tell you to jump. Jump into Love! Jump into passion! Jump into purpose! Question why you've always done it that way. Live with Love at the forefront more often than not.

No one expects perfection. We're only asking you to give yourself a choice: Love or Fear.

Collectively we are like a pot of soup. Alone, one flavor could not touch the complexity of all the ingredients coming together. If, as a collective consciousness movement, we bring our best "flavors" forward through self-realization, we create a more abundant life for everyone. You have been tainted by the ego and conditioned beliefs. Your ego holds back your essence by expecting you to identify with stories of who you are, and conditioned beliefs are stories we've created around Love, Fear, attachment, and security.

These patterns begin to form in the early years of Life, typically guided by parents, and continue to develop through our social exposure. If you're the carrot in the soup, first, you must let go of the conditioned belief that you must be buried. You cannot be buried in the soil if you're going to participate in the party. You're meant to provide nutrients to the world - if you stay where you are, you'll never fulfill your purpose.

Once you've been pulled from the darkness, you'll still be covered in dirt, aka the ego. We fear if we let go, we'll lose a part of who we are. You're right: once you let go of the pain, you no longer get to identify with it. You know no one wants dirt in their soup. It's time to let that shit go. When we bring our flavors together with the purest intentions, we create an enriched life and raise the collective vibration.

Our mission is to come together with Love at the forefront of our path. Through the stories that created our unique experiences, Love for self, community, and oneness, navigated itself to the limelight. We share our story to help you step into your power. We acknowledge the oneness within each soul. The illusion of separation is quite clearly a delusion. We see a world of unity. Individually raising our vibration affects the entire energy field - we create Peace, Love, and Unity through all. We choose to change our paths, to show that it can be done. We call to you through this guide to choose Love. We don't want to change you; you already have everything you need. If you're reading this, you're ready to align with your purpose. You're the individual we wrote these words for.

THE BLUEPRINT

I never had any intention of coming up with these ten principles, let alone this book. I believe when you're living in the flow that opportunities are presented to you, and only from this flow state are you able to receive them. One day I was getting ready for a speaking event, and I usually speak from the heart; I use whatever downloads. This time, I decided to write what I was going to talk about, and this is how these ten principles came to be. The date started to get closer, and for whatever reason, I chose not to use these principles as speaking points. I ultimately shelved them and just spoke from my heart as usual.

Fast forward one year, and I'm watching a YouTube video on speaking, and the question was asked, "what do I give my audience to take away from my speaking events?" Well, I thought to myself, "just my words and my energy". We all know words come and go, and energy always changes forms. Just like that, a light bulb went off! I decided I was going to elaborate on those ten principles and create a book that's easy to read, practical, and created with Love. Now, I can give my audience something tangible and also from the heart. You never know what you're capable of until you surrender to the best version of your highest self. God. Are you ready for this, the journey? If so, here is the blueprint:

10 Principles for Transformation

LOVE

Love is the most powerful force in the Universe. Love converts enemies to friends. Love turns dark to light. Love is the ultimate Alchemist.

GRATITUDE

Gratitude is the key to living in harmony. It is being thankful for what is already yours.

MINDFULNESS AND MEDITATION

In the short term, you'll deal with stress in a much more effective way. Long term, you'll put yourself on the fast track to living your purpose. Make time.

CONSTRUCTIVE MINDSET

It's time to drop the self-doubt. You can do what you desire. Life is no longer happening 'to you' it's happening 'for you.' Choose your disposition.

CONSISTENCY

A regular practice of healthy habits turns into life-changing events.

BE PRESENT

A focused mind eliminates stress and anxiety. Live in peace and choose now.

SERVE
Find your gifts and share them with joy. We're here for one another.

FAILURE
Reality check! Failure doesn't exist. You don't fail; you learn, and you grow. You only fail when you stop trying.

BE PROACTIVE
Work towards something rather than waiting for it to happen.

STEPPING OUT OF FEAR
Fear is the absence of Love, built from insecurities; it's a façade, a perceived force that can paralyze progress or push you to success. The reality is, it's just smoke; there is no fire. Let's break it down!

THE LOVE FACTOR

"Darkness cannot drive out darkness; only light can do that. Hate cannot drive out hate; only Love can do that."
Martin Luther King

"The more motivated by love, the more fearless & free your actions will be."
Dalai Lama

PRINCIPLE 1 - LOVE

Love's high vibe

As we realize deep within our core, all we see is Love. Love is the highest form of vibration. It spreads through a smile, a kind word, or a genuine touch. Have you ever been kissed on the forehead, right between your eyebrows? Did you feel that connection?! We have an understanding of sound waves, light waves, and physical shifts in the ocean. We have created a habit of relying on our five senses to validate truth, missing the energy and vibrations that cannot easily be explained.

All emotions carry vibration. When acting out of Love, the vibration is so high you can levitate, but getting caught in the low frequencies of guilt, shame, or judgment might alter your timeline. This Low frequency is living from the "basement view." Deciding to operate from Love leaves no room for the low vibrations to exist. No longer is it an option to remain at a low frequency. When operating on a high level, the dips of discontent will no longer take control.

Inevitably, you will slip from the elevated state of Love, and when you do, like the ocean waves, simply let it come and go. Welcome to the penthouse of Life! I want to offer you these steps for elevating your vibration and state of being, and move to the 'penthouse view'. When you fall into a low vibe of Fear, anger, guilt, judgment, or scarcity:

STEPS FOR ELEVATING YOUR VIBE

LISTEN
Listening to an uplifting song is positive energy in and positive energy out. My favorite reggae artist can bring me right up to the feeling of unity and peace.

EAT SOME NOURISHING FOOD
Healthy body! Healthy mind! Healthy soul! As a vegan, I enjoy high vibrational foods, such as my favorite fruits.

TAKE A REST
Listen to your body; it's speaking to you. Rest is the key to recovery and healing - it rejuvenates and uplifts my spirits.

MEDITATE
Take 5 minutes, set intentions, and breathe through the tension. Focused breathing, relaxation, and concentration are the keys to bringing me right back to the present moment, and that creates right-thinking - and right-thinking raises my vibe.

TAKE A WALK

Take a walk and find something that makes you smile. When I need to redirect my focus, I often go for a walk, usually in nature - seeing the birds, trees, water, etc. It has a calming effect and gives me a reboot. An excellent vigorous workout releases endorphins, feeling your physical strength evolve. My vigorous workout used to be heavyweights at the gym, but because of the COVID-19 pandemic, the workout facilities are closed so I will go for a bike ride up to the lake, only about 2.5 miles each way, do 500 pushups, and jump right back on my bike and come home. That usually does the trick.

POSITIVE VIEWING STIMULATION

Watch a 5-minute motivational video; it doesn't have to be long, it can be short, quick and to the point. My choice of motivational videos changes from day to day. My preference is spirituality, by nature, but I enjoy "rah-rah" videos, too.

HUGS

Hug someone you love - touch releases oxytocin. I enjoy hugging my babies and my wife. It not only releases oxytocin, but it deepens your connection with that person.

CREATIVITY

Get artistic — paint, draw, sculpt, write... be expressive as an author. Writing takes me to a flow state where I'm living in the now, the zone, which elevates my vibe tremendously.

WHAT WILL BE, WILL BE

Let go, breathe, accept what is. Letting go is part of the healing process. First, you must recognize what needs to be processed and healed before the letting go can take place. All this comes with practice.

LOVE WITHOUT CONDITIONS = TRUE LOVE

"Love without conditions will not only heal you, but it will heal the world."
Monk Coleman

"We are not held back by the love we didn't receive in the past, but by the love we're not extending in the present."
Marianne Williamson

If you see it as possible, you're right. Unconditional Love is transformative. It sees past judgment & knows no limits. Love cannot be contained because it is who you are. We've been taught to use the word LOVE rather loosely. We love our cars, our food, our spouse, and our best friend. Though these are forms of admiration, typically, they're surrounded by conditions. Unconditional Love does not need permission. This vibration looks past the hatred aimed towards the color of one's skin and recognizes the undesirable acts as misguided ignorance. It sees 'God' within all people and has no attachments to what is 'supposed to be.' Saying 'I love you, but...' creates conditions; the 'but' negates everything that came before it. To be altruistic (showing unselfish concern for others' wellbeing) is the most authentic reflection of Love. When you operate from this level, it's not just your heart that reaps the benefit. Unconditional Love is overarching. It encompasses all Love, including self-love and forgiveness.

3 KEY INSIGHTS ON UNCONDITIONAL LOVE

PRACTICE UNDERSTANDING
Each person is in their process of transformation. It is far from your responsibility to deem anything as 'good' or 'bad' - accept and love.

SET BOUNDARIES
It's okay to say no. Its okay to eliminate toxic relationships and still have Love for the person. Your wellbeing is a part of loving unconditionally.

FAIL

Allow yourself to be bad at Love. Watch for judgment and anger. Recognize low vibrations and choose how you'll move with them next time. Unconditional Love is a continuous effort until enlightenment occurs. The ultimate goal is self-actualization. When you slip & recognize it, you get to choose growth.

SELF-LOVE 101

We have been programmed from day one to understand Love; our upbringing and social circle shape how we view the world. The pattern is taught by people who likely have never questioned their existence and can be hard to shift (especially for those experienced in years). When you follow the same patterns, it becomes a deeply ingrained habit, like sleepwalking through Life. When seeking validation through material items, or having an over-emphasis on appearance, maybe the NEED to be the best, we can create a false identity rather than living our truth.

We seek approval from others because we can't find it within ourselves. There is no need to seek it; just realize it. You are Love. Look in the mirror & see God in you. Realize the miracle that you are. Understand you are deserving of Love. This is not an inflated sense of self. You were born with this status. An infant rarely considers the thoughts of how they'll be cared for. They scream out until their needs are met. Self-love is putting your wellbeing at the top of importance. It's creating boundaries with the people you love and people that are hard to love.

We all have choices as to what direction we want to go in any given situation. We can go the fear route or the love route. One is the truth, and one is false. I've realized Love is who we are, our highest self, so whenever I fail to understand who I am, I'm quickly reminded of my true nature by tapping into the Love that's never absent, by looking inside, where it's always welcoming me back home.

6 PRINCIPLES ON SELF-LOVE

CHOOSE GRATITUDE
Every morning, express gratitude for opening your eyes. Thank your body for restoring you through the night. Thank you for showing up and doing the best you can. Gratitude is the precursor of Love.

PRACTICE ACCEPTANCE
Here is your public service announcement: YOU CAN STOP BEING SO HARD ON YOURSELF. Forgive yourself for mistakes, and let go. Choose growth through all circumstances and form the habit of loving every part of you.

SET BOUNDARIES

Your emotional state is your responsibility. Draw a line with negative self-talk. Choose when and how you interact with people deemed as toxic. The reality is, their opinion has nothing to do with you.

MAKE A PLAN

Self-love is a habit; post sticky notes with affirmations on every door in your home, send yourself a reminder text that reads, 'You Are Amazing for...', celebrate your superpowers. Find a way to remember how wonderful you are.

LISTEN TO YOUR BODY

It's speaking to you. It will tell you when it's tired. It will tense up when you're anxious. It will be at ease when you're at peace. Pay attention and honor it. Be unapologetic in accepting you.

SELF-LOVE = FORGIVENESS

Let go of what concerns you. Holding toxic energy prevents you from the peace you deserve. Holding onto resentment, hurt, and pain is a choice. Forgiveness, along with gratitude, is the main component in propelling you towards a purpose-filled existence. This is Love. Forgiveness can be difficult but know it's not for them. Coming from a place of Love, it's easy to recognize the struggle in someone. We see that they fall to conditioned beliefs, too. We do the best we can with the level of consciousness we have.

Self-forgiveness can be slightly more challenging. We create stories of how things should be. We hold onto pain because if we let it go, we release a part of our identity (this is ego). You're in a beautiful place when you recognize there are times you wish you could get a 're-do.' You've grown in understanding - you get to choose differently next time. Forgiveness is the path to freedom.

The question at hand is how to find forgiveness. Do you feel hurt? Anger? Resentment? Abandonment? Do you have negative self-talk? If the answer is yes, then here are my principles to help you rise up: My biggest challenge with forgiveness was forgiving myself for all the things I've done when I wasn't in alignment.

STEPS FOR FORGIVENESS

BE WHERE YOU ARE
Listen to your heart; it's speaking to you. Emotions show up for a reason. Love, hurt, guilt, or shame; they're all messengers. The first step is to identify what emotions show up. Once you've named it, you have a choice.

BE KIND
Be kind and act out of Love. Hold yourself with the same loving kindness you would give to your most beloved connection. We're all doing the best we can.

BE PRESENT
Accept that there is only now. Bringing the past into the present moment brings the pain into this moment. You carry pain and miss the perfection of now.

CHOOSE A PEACEFUL EXISTENCE
Use pain to propel you forward. Stop playing the 'Poor me' game. Everything is happening "for you", not "to you."

In my Life, I choose forgiveness as my motto. I now understand forgiveness; not only is it a form of Love, but it's the pathway to freedom. Until I started forgiving my past and everything in it, I was still anchored to those old, low vibrational energies and experiences. Whenever something comes up from my past that triggers me, I'll feel it thoroughly and then allow it to go. There are layers of trauma in our history that we may not even be aware of until something or someone triggers that in you. This is the perfect opportunity to forgive, let go, and heal.

AN ATTITUDE FOR GRATITUDE

"*Every moment a million miracles are happening around you: a flower blossoming, a bird tweeting, a bee humming, a raindrop falling, a snowflake wafting along with the clear evening air. There's magic everywhere. If you learn how to live it, Life is nothing short of a daily miracle.*"
Sadhguru

"*Feeling gratitude and not expressing it is like wrapping a present and not giving it.*"
William Arthur Ward

PRINCIPLE 2 - GRATITUDE

Have you ever gotten the, "If you don't like it, I'll take it back!"? My mother often put me in check. How quickly some things come and go. That was a life lesson; thanks, Mom! When you're grateful for what you have, you end up with more! The opposite is the truth as well. We all have witnessed a person who "has it all", but never has "enough". This person typically lacks a level of gratitude. Likely with a scarcity mindset, they cling to things that don't matter, yet they're still unhappy.

The compelling part, people with few possessions can lead to a more abundant life. Merely due to mindset. With an understanding that Life itself is a gift. Breath, family, Love, and ability; we have everything we need. Gratitude comes down to feeling the thorn on the rose and still recognizing its beauty; seeing the pain and saying thank you. Recognize that each step in your path shapes you and allows you to realize your core (Love). Gratitude is losing the victim mentality of 'why me' and shifting it to 'use me.'

GRATITUDE 101 - 5 STEPS FOR GRATITUDE

JOURNAL
Write in it often (daily is a good practice). It can be a simple list or an elaborate letter. Write about the things that make you smile.

WAKE UP IN APPRECIATION
As soon as you open your eyes, say 'Thank you.' Repeat those two words. Don't search for gratitude. Just keep saying 'Thank You' until gratitude trickles in.

THANK SOMEONE OUT LOUD
Be intentional. Make it known how vital they are to your existence. It's the little things that make big things.

STAY PRESENT
Quit bringing the stories of old pains (depression) or future fears (anxiety) into the now. At this very moment, you are safe, whole, and peaceful. Slow down and smell the flowers. Look at the birds, see the shapes in the clouds, and feel the sun on your skin. Say thank you for those sensations.

RECOGNIZE PAIN AS A GIFT
Your story holds superpowers. Choose a life that is happening 'for you' not 'to you.'

At the beginning of my marriage, I wanted everything the way I wanted it, and if it didn't live up to my standards, I would have a problem with it. See, my problem was I was focusing on the perceived shortcomings of my partner. When I started to live with gratitude in my life, I shifted my focus and realized all the beautiful attributes she had, and I became so grateful that I realized there were no shortcomings, just a lack of gratitude on my part.

BE STILL AND KNOW

"Silence is essential. We need silence just as much as we need air, just as much as plants need light. If our minds are crowded with words and thoughts, there is no space for us."
Thich Nhat Hanh

"If you just sit and observe, you will see how restless your mind is. If you try to calm it, it only makes it worse, but over time it does calm, and when it does, there's room to hear more subtle things – that's when your intuition starts to blossom, and you start to see things more clearly and be in the present more. Your mind just slows down, and you see a tremendous expanse of the moment. You see so much more than you could see before."
Steve Jobs

"When you make genuine contact with your inner spirit, there is an inner joy, an inner peace that takes over."
Michael Beckwith

PRINCIPLE 3 - MINDFULNESS, aka MEDITATION

Take a moment to stop and breathe. It has more benefits than you'd expect! It literally grows your brain and leads you to a more compassionate/love-filled life. What more could you ask for?! It reduces stress, increases your emotional intelligence, slows ageing, boosts your immune system, increases serotonin & dopamine, and gives you a sense of oneness.

People fear meditation, assuming their thoughts run too wild to sit in silence. If you are too busy with meditation, you are too busy not to meditate. We tend to fall victim to circumstance and can lose power over our lives. Meditation navigates us back towards harmony. As soon as you stop giving so much attention to these wandering thoughts, they dissipate. When you stop taking them so seriously, they lose their power. Buddhists call this indecisive, unsettled thinking "Monkey Mind." A thinking pattern that swings from one thought to the next. The monkey mind can be tamed. Take a breath.

Meditation was always something I've heard about, but I never really knew what it was. I never knew of the transformational power that it held. Sitting in meditation over the years enabled me to face my demons finally and realize those "demons" were here for my growth. Sitting in stillness allowed me to get reacquainted with my true self.

MEDITATION 101
5 STEPS FOR MINDFULNESS

MEDITATION IS NOT...

Voodoo, evil, a trance state, or running from reality.

MEDITATION IS NOT A PASS OR FAIL ACTIVITY

It's called a practice. You'll find the way that works best for you.

SET A TIMER

The Fear of getting stuck in silence forever happens. Start with 5 minutes and make a slow progression towards sitting for more extended periods of time.

MEDITATION DOESN'T MEAN SITTING IN SILENCE

Meditation is a go-to practice (and gives you a direct connection to your inner knowing). Taking a shower, cooking a meal, creating art, lifting weights, or taking a hike - become fully immersed in these activities and create a meditative state.

IT'S HELPFUL TO CONCENTRATE ON A PARTICULAR SENSATION.

The coolness of the inhale, or the warmth of the exhale.

The rise and fall of your abdomen or subtle calming pulse of your heart.

Having a sensation to go back to acts as a guide when your thoughts drift.

BEST PRACTICES - 6 STEPS FOR MEDITATION

The keyword is practice. Recognize every time you sit; it is perfect. Don't try to change it. Don't try to focus harder or to stop your thoughts. It's a process of patience, falling off, and gently guiding yourself back. There is no wrong way to meditate. Here are brief instructions on how you might sit.

FIND A QUIET PLACE AND SET A TIMER
This is not necessary, but it is helpful for relaxation. The most important part is you feel safe, and will not be disturbed.

SIT
On a chair or the floor. It's helpful to elevate your hips with a pillow to align your spine & take the pressure off your lower back. Find a place to ground in. You could try lying down.

CLOSE YOUR EYES & BREATHE
Notice your breath. Get balanced. Sit upright to attain attention. Closing your eyes allows the nervous system to slip into a rest & relax state, enabling you to go deeper.

TAKE A DEEP INHALATION

Followed by a FULL exhalation. Do this three times, fully expanding your lungs with each breath. Then fall into your natural rhythm of breathing.

START YOUR TIMER.

COME BACK TO YOUR BREATH WHEN YOUR MIND STEPS IN.

Mindfulness is the main reason you are reading these words right now. I first had to dive headfirst into mindfulness in order to have made this transformation in my life that allowed me to write this book. If you are reading this book, you most likely have had your experience with mindfulness and meditation.

A CENTERED MIND

"Quiet the mind, and the soul will speak."
Ma Jaya Sati Bhagavati

"I've learned that no matter what happens, or how bad it seems today, life does go on, and it will be better tomorrow."
Maya Angelou

"If you change the way you look at things, the things you look at change."
Wayne Dyer

PRINCIPLE 4 - CONSTRUCTIVE MINDSET

Tools, like this book, help you to engage in a constructive outlook. Not everything has to be positive. Part of the human experience is learning from pain. Instinctively, if you touch something hot, you're not going to touch it again because your body has learned a lesson. When you see the pains of Life as lessons, you get to grow. Now that you are in a state of knowing, you heal, and no longer do you get to complain.

No longer are you losing in any way. You are winning, or you are learning - the downside no longer exists. When you go in expecting the worst case, you will receive it. You are a self-fulfilling prophecy. When you claim 'bad days', it's what you'll get. When you claim abundance, healthy relationships, & Love, these will come. Every day is a chance to claim your power. You don't have to be positive all of the time - it feels pretty good, though. It's SUPER easy to justify negative thought patterns. Our ego loves to claim these painful stories because it gives us a sense of identity. It's time for you to claim your power back. You get to rewrite your story.

PRINCIPLES FOR A CONSTRUCTIVE MINDSET

CHANGE YOUR CIRCLE
Surround yourself with people who are in alignment with where you're going. It›s time for quality time with quality people.

WATCH YOUR THOUGHTS
What you think, you become. Start to turn away negative self-talk. Out of Love, say, 'Hey, I see you & I love you, but I no longer use words like that. I refuse to claim it.' Release that story.

STOP JUSTIFYING YOUR JUDGMENT
Just stop. What someone does with their life choices are none of your business.

NO COMPLAINING
No complaining ever. This hard rule takes practice. Just because I said no complaining ever, doesn't mean it›s not going to happen, but that's the goal. Don't get down on yourself if the transformation doesn›t happen right away. It is all about being more conscious of your thoughts and speech because they matter.

CELEBRATE DAILY

Find something. Big, small, short, tall, have a love for it all!

ONLY CONSUME POSITIVE MEDIA

What you think, you become. What you put in, you get out. It's easy to see on a physical level, and the same holds true on a mental level.

Stop protecting your negative life choices or story. Claim the beauty and abundance that is yours. You are whole and perfect where you are. Now drive after what is yours. Energy flows where attention goes. I've noticed in my own life when I'm really on my game; I have laser focus when it comes to where I place my energy. And what you place your energy on determines your mindset.

STICK WITH IT

"When people see commitments are met with consistency, they tend to develop trust."
Khalid Imran

"What makes a publishing house great? The easy answer is consistency with which it produces books of value over a lengthy period of time."
Robert Gottlieb

PRINCIPLE 5 - CONSISTENCY

To form any new habit, you have to do it repeatedly. As you repeat lifestyle changes, they become second nature. Congratulations! You have begun to rewire a new path. Most of our behaviors and thoughts are subconscious. Meaning they happen without much effort on our part.

Trying to evolve the way we move through the world, we have to be head-strong through the process. It's about trying and "failing" and trying again. It's about repeating that cycle until you get it right two times in a row, three times - then it's natural. Fear may come, and you might slip from your path. You win as soon as you notice. Now you get to choose. You are unlimited potential. For you, there is no ceiling as to where you can go. The 'ups & downs' are part of the wave of Life. Consistency is what elevates your skills to navigate the waves with grace. Stop winging it and move with intention.

5 STEPS FOR CONSISTENCY

PLAN
Set a schedule for when you'll go to the gym. Set the alarm for when you'll meditate. Set a time to disconnect. Stop winging it, and act in a calculated way.

KEEP YOUR WORD

Do what you say you will. You'll create trust within yourself; your word becomes bond. Now when you claim it to be true, you believe it.

ACCOUNTABILITY

Own it all: good, bad, or ugly. Be honest with yourself about your commitment. Ask a friend to help you. Stay on track.

USE TOOLS

With no shame. Post affirmations everywhere. Listen to positive podcasts. Elevate your mood, feed your soul with music. Break a sweat and celebrate it. Find people who align with your mission & turn to them for guidance.

CREATE A VISION

A ship without a captain is going nowhere fast. Define what you're driving towards and how you'll achieve it.

- Set the stage!
- Be clear about your desired destination!
- Dream big!
- Be forward-thinking!
- Make it achievable!
- Enjoy the process!

Stop taking life so seriously. Find humor in the things that are supposed to derail you, as a natural professional physique bodybuilder it's hard to find a more appropriate word that will take you to that next level than consistency. When I'm consistent day in and day out, the results are inevitable. This is true for anything else you want to achieve in your life.

HELLO, ARE YOU AWAKE?

"Always say "yes" to the present moment. What could be more futile, more insane than to create inner resistance to what already is? What could be more insane than to oppose life itself, which is now and always now? Surrender to what is. Say "yes" to Life — and see how life suddenly starts working for you rather than against you."

Eckhart Tolle

"Don't ruin a good today by thinking of a bad yesterday. Let it go!"

Russel Simons

PRINCIPLE 6 - BE PRESENT

Pain-bodies exist in the past or future; they are rarely in the present moment. Yes, there are exceptions, but in this very moment upon evaluation, you're likely doing just fine. You're breathing, your heart is pumping, you don't feel threatened, and you are safe. Remember that time you wish you could get a 'do-over.' Had you said the right thing, or done it differently, the outcome may be altered and the 'end result' perhaps better.

Wishing away the past does not make it go away. It brings the story to the present moment. We don't have to feel that pain anymore, but we choose to bring it to this moment, choosing to live the pain again. In some cases, the opposite is true, reminiscing on the 'good ole days,' wishing away your present moment, rather than reveling in its excellence. Neither scenario serves you. It's easy to get caught in 'what-ifs' based on past experience. We induce anxiety by creating a story of what will be, rather than experiencing what is.

This story of Fear calls the pain into our experience. There is a fine line between anxiety and excitement. It's a simple mindset shift. Acting out of fear creates anxiety. Embracing what's to come without expectations creates excitement.

PRINCIPLES FOR WAKING UP
TO THE PRESENT MOMENT

FORGIVE & RELEASE YOUR PAST
Stop dwelling on your story. You've grown. Now let go.

DISCONNECT
Step away from distractions. Indulge in what's in front of you. A home-cooked meal or a redwood grove, a run or a walk - find your peace and completely immerse yourself in it. Touch, feel, smell, taste, be. Don't change it, just love it.

MEDITATE
Practice until being present is a rule, not an exception. Claim a mindful existence so often that it's odd for you to be elsewhere.

FIND LITTLE JOYS
They make up the big things in life. Smile every chance you get. Notice something that touches your heart. Let them bring you joy.

CREATE REMINDERS
Bring yourself into the present moment with a note on your bathroom mirror, or put a meditative ornament in your workspace. Reminded yourself over and over until it's natural.

I watched so much of my life pass me by because I was not present to partake in it. Yes, I was physically there, but I was not wholly present. Being present today is one of the most beautiful gifts that I have given myself. Life is beautiful when you actually experience it.

THE COLLECTIVE

"One of the things I keep learning is that the secret of being happy is doing things for other people."
Dick Gregory

"Grant me the courage to serve others; for in service there is true life"
Cesar Chavez

PRINCIPLE 7 - ACTS OF SERVICE

We are here to uplift one another collectively. We each bring a gift, and our duty is to identify how to use it. Your soul is connected to the people you interact with. Acts of service are acts of Love. Those acts of Love turn you towards a purpose-driven life. As you find what makes you happy, you understand where you shine out and how you can use your gift. When you've identified how you best contribute - time, emotional support, strength, intellect, patience - you can get to the action. Start with simple things: hold the door open, give a compliment, share a smile. These acts reap benefits for all parties. Move to living your purpose and using your gifts to spread the love-vibe that you are.

PRINCIPLE FOR GIVING MORE

GIVE YOUR TIME
Give your neighbor a ride to the grocery store,
volunteer with a local organization,
read to your grandchild,
swing a hammer,
tutor a student,
clean house. Many elderly and people have physical limitations that can use a helping hand.

Keep in mind; your time is your most valuable resource. Giving it is precious.

GIVE YOUR EXTRAS
Clothes, food, toys, tools, space, money — these resources can be replenished. Separate your 'needs' from your 'wants.' You likely can live a more minimalistic life & share your wealth.

GIVE YOUR EAR
You don't need the answers, nor do you have to find the solution, you just have to give space with a lack of judgment.

GIVE YOUR SMILE
When you smile, you trigger them to smile back. You both just got a feel-good shot of endorphins with that small act.

Whatever you give, give it from your heart. Do not expect reciprocation. Act from Love, and you will receive that energy back. If this concept is unfamiliar to you, don't be too hard on yourself - it was unfamiliar to me, too. When I finally realized I got more joy out of giving than I did receiving, it all made sense.

THERE ARE NONE

"I will not lose, for even in defeat, there's a valuable lesson learned, so it evens up for me."
Jay Z

"Never surrender, it's all about the faith you got; don't ever stop, just push it 'till you hit the top, and if you drop, at least you know you gave your all to be true to you, that way you can never fail."
Tupac

PRINCIPLE 8 - FAILURE

By definition, failure is a lack of success. Until you have accepted failure as your reality, it does not exist. Failure can only be present when you stop trying, and until then, you're still working on perfecting whatever you're choosing. In Major League Baseball, an elite batting average is .300. Anything above that is considered extraordinary. That means for every 10 times at bat, they hit the ball 3 times. That is a 30% success rate or a 70% failure rate.

When we think of these athletes, failure is far from what comes to mind. Perception is everything. When we look at these 'above the rest' athletes, we only see their success. When you evaluate your performance, where does your focus lie? Can you see all of your success before you focus on your areas of improvement? Can you reframe your 'miss at-bat' as a learning opportunity and pivot to a growth mindset? Now that you know, it's a choice.

INSIGHTS FOR A GROWTH MINDSET

BE AWARE OF SELF-TALK
The way you talk to yourself matters. If you deem yourself as not good enough or unworthy, you will call that to your existence. Identify your superpowers and celebrate your worthiness. Be your own biggest cheerleader.

USE YOUR 'FAILURE'
Use your failure as a guide! Look at what did not go well and how you might shift your approach next time. Learn and grow.

DON'T BE FIXATED ON THE OUTCOME
Use the flow of your plot-twists as guides towards the direction you need to go. It's the journey, not the destination.

GROW
Get comfortable with being uncomfortable. Muscle growth requires you to tear down before you build up. Learning to ride a bike, you'll undoubtedly scrape your knee. You did not fail, but you're not going to lose your balance like that again!

WORDS MATTER

Failure, loss, defeat, inadequacy - these words are no longer a part of your vocabulary. It's not an option. As you become more conscious, you start to catch yourself, and when you do, you can shift your self sabotaging pattern. Until then, here are some tips to help you get there quicker.

- Have a friend hold you accountable for your speech.
- Think before you speak.
- Practice by using positive affirmations.
- When you catch yourself, immediately replace the disempowering word with an empowering word.

We create our reality based on the thoughts we have and the emotions we experience. How do you choose to see yourself? Throughout my life, I've "failed" at almost everything that I've ever tried, which then turned my Life, in my opinion, to a complete failure. As I look back at my "failures," I've realized that I needed every one of those experiences to be where I am today. Failure now is just a learning opportunity.

ACTION JACKSON

"Do what you have to do, to do what you want to do."
Denzel Washington

"A winner is a dreamer who never gives up."
Nelson Mandela

PRINCIPLE 9 - TAKE ACTION

There is a 'knowledge gap' between knowing what to do and actually doing it. It's time to stop sitting back & letting Life happen to you. Start choosing your path. Start choosing your happiness. Complacency is the opposite of productivity. It's also the opposite of abundance.

It's time for you to step into your power without reservation. You've been conditioned and told what to do thus far. Some of those patterns sabotage your greatness. You get to choose to address the ones that no longer serve you. As you push through the boundaries, the discomfort becomes addicting. You recognize when you step into that uncomfortable zone; you're growing. The challenge of climbing the mountain gets you to the peak, and you'll soon recognize that uncomfortable sensation was simply the growing pains. Taking the first step towards starting something new may not feel pleasant, but it's necessary.

PRINCIPLES FOR ELEVATING PRODUCTIVITY

DO ONE THING EVERY DAY
Baby steps - they'll get you there. Remember, the small steps create significant steps.

NOW IS THE TIME
It's never going to be the 'right time.' If you can do it now, do it. It will take you double the time and brainpower to put it down and pick it back up.

PRIORITIZE
Choose the tasks with a high payout. Execute those first.

BE ACCOUNTABLE
Do what you say you're going to do. Find a coach or a partner to help you succeed. Check in daily to make sure you're executing your goals.

BOUNCE BACK
You will fall. How are you going to rebound? You don't have the option of failure anymore, so dust yourself off and keep going.

I've learned a lot of lessons throughout my journey back to self, but it always seemed like something was missing when it came to manifestation and fully embracing my purpose. I was afraid to take action.

This was the final step to manifesting my dreams. The time to take action is now.

"Fear – the biggest dream killer, goal killer, and #1 limiting factor that keeps us from the Life we want if we succumb to it."
Monk Coleman

"So many of us choose our path out of fear disguised as practicality. What we want seems impossibly out of reach, so we never dare to ask the Universe for it. I'm proof that you can ask the Universe for it."
Jim Carrey

PRINCIPLE 10 -
FEAR "STEPPING OUT AND INTO LOVE"

Fear is normal. It comes as a survival tactic to protect against perceived dangers. When you recognize something as a threat, you're likely going to step out of that situation. The familiar fight or flight sensation comes in, and you act. No emotion should be shrugged off as unimportant. They're messengers and should be treated as such. You take power away from these 'negative' emotions when you perceive them as a memo.

Unfortunately, our ancient brains do not know the difference between running from a lion and asking for a promotion. We perceive a threat, so our breathing shallows, our body sweats, our heart races, and we forget our words. Fear can be debilitating: for some, it's public speaking, others its rejection, or even reverting to old habits. It all comes from creating a story of what the future will hold. Fear is waiting for something terrible to happen, calling the poor outcome into your future. What you think, you become. Think negative thoughts, you get negative results.

My personal experience with fear is one that I'm still working on. Fear again comes, except now I have a different relationship with it. I no longer run from it using alcohol and being involved in addictive, reckless behavior. I can now sit with it, process it, and allow it to run its course.

There are three main fears: Fear of judgment, Fear of failing, and Fear of pain. The first two are no longer a part of your journey.

What others think of you has nothing to do with you. Failing is no longer an option (you don't fail, you learn).

Fear of pain can be real - if you are physically threatened, use that sensation as a signal of survival.

Remember, not all physical pain is negative. During fitness training, you have to break down your muscles before you can build them.

Luckily, when you jump to the other side of Fear, magic happens. When you get comfortable with being uncomfortable, you move mountains.

PRINCIPLES FOR STEPPING OUT OF FEAR

CONTROL YOUR BREATHING
When a lion is chasing you, you're not going to stop, gather your thoughts, and slow your breathing pattern. The intentional breath tricks your body into being at ease.

CONTROL YOUR THOUGHTS
Much like breathing, when you're in a panic and switch your thought patterns to that which brings you joy, your body resets to ease.

FACE THEM

Look your Fear in the eye. Determine if it is serving you or hindering you. Make a choice.

VISUALIZE SUCCESS

See a successful outcome. What you think, you become. Think positive, receive positive.

BE PREPARED

Practice the speech, become more educated, and assemble the resources to be successful. Cover your bases, so you're ready to pivot if needed.

WHAT I'VE LEARNED

"LIVING IN FAITH, NOT BY HOPE"

This book intends to remind you of the greatness and unlimited potential that you are. I want to give you five "takes-aways" and reminders.

1. We're all on a journey to identify and live our purpose.
2. We're all here to share our gifts with the world.
3. We're all here to find peace in our lives whilst living it to the fullest.
4. We're all here to raise the collective consciousness.
5. We're all here to live a life of Love.

Your limits are due to your limiting beliefs. Shift to faith and watch the change take place. Fear, whew. I struggled with Fear for so long due to my insecurities. I felt compelled a few years back to make a Facebook live video on my eight years of sobriety journey, but I was terrified. I knew this would help people, but I was concerned with how I would be perceived. Thirty years prior, I had never spoken in front of people, live, or on the internet. I built up the courage to do it and jumped in. I received such a positive response and received direct messages with questions I could answer. It was amazing. From that video, I was also contacted by a woman who asked me to come to LA and speak at her house, and she'd pay me - before I could talk myself out of it, I immediately said YES! I was scared, but I knew I had to step through Fear once again. The funny and amazing thing is, as soon as I stepped through Fear, my new career/purpose began to rise - like a phoenix rising from the ashes.

I always give credit to Teresa Jordan, the woman who asked me to speak, and the legendary musician/singer Lonnie Jordan (lead singer for the iconic band WAR and Teresa's husband) for being the catalyst for my speaking career. Success is what happens when you put fear in its place. It no longer stops you from living in your truth. A lot of times, the things you're most frightened of is the thing that's your greatest superpower. Through the ups and downs, trust everything is working exactly as it should. Living in faith allows you to lose the victim mentality. You cultivate trust and move forward in power.

We comfortably live by faith when it comes to the sun rising in the morning, or continuing to breathe through the night. We forget that we can choose to walk in confidence when it comes to obtaining more and dreaming bigger. The power is already within you. All you have to do is trust that you are worthy. By hoping it will work out, you're putting the power in someone else's hands. You are DIVINE. You are WORTHY. You are POWERFUL.

ABOUT THE AUTHOR

Monk Coleman is the author of *Love over Fear – A Guide to Peace and Purpose.* A guide to letting go of belief systems and connecting to a higher state of being.

Monk is a graduate of the University of Holistic Theology.

He is a Transformational Coach, Public Speaker, Personal Trainer and a 3x Pro Natural Physique Bodybuilder.

His coaching services can be found on all social media platforms at **www.monketernal.com**.

He based his coaching program on his own experience with dealing and healing from alcoholism, poverty, depression and dysfunctional relationships.

Monk has taken his years of experience and created a life of service with love at the forefront.

CPSIA information can be obtained
at www.ICGtesting.com
Printed in the USA
BVHW061015140121
597841BV00010B/459